Drawing DoodleLoops

Creative Whole Language Activities for Beginning Writers

written and illustrated by
Sandy Baker

Copyright © 1994, Good Apple

ISBN No. 0-86653-789-9

Printing No. 987654321

Good Apple
1204 Buchanan St., Box 299
Carthage, IL 62321-0299

Paramount Publishing

A Word About *Drawing DoodleLoops*

The DoodleLoops included in this book are a unique learning tool. Particularly if used daily, they stimulate creative thinking and can actually teach creativity. If used over a period of time, DoodleLoops promote divergent thinking, broaden the children's perceptions, and naturally lead into the writing process. They can be used to teach a multitude of skills, from simple creative expression through drawing activities to storytelling, creative writing, language arts skills, and spelling. DoodleLoops involve little or no teacher preparation and offer incredible results!

How to Begin

1. Use a demonstration Drawing DoodleLoop (page 1) to introduce the DoodleLoop concept.

2. Make four copies of this page. Hold one copy right side up in front of the group.

Tell the children that you are going to add lines and shapes to the drawing in order to create a new picture.

3. Post the DoodleLoop in clear view of all of the children, and make a simple drawing such as this one:

Tell the children that the triangle has now turned into a clown's hat.

4. Display a second △ drawing, again right side up. Now ask the children to offer suggestions as to what this triangle can become, such as a rocket, the roof of a house, the sail of a boat, etc. Illustrate one of their suggestions.

Samples:

5. Display a third △ drawing. This time turn the drawing upside down and ask what the shape now suggests. Accept all answers and illustrate one.

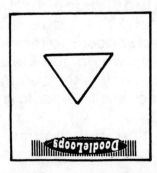

Published by Good Apple © 1994, Sandy Baker GA1483

If the children need prompting, offer one of the following suggestions:

6. Display the last △ drawing. This time turn it sideways. Ask what the shape suggests now. Once again, accept all answers and illustrate one.

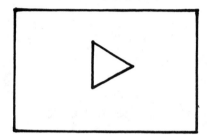

If the children still need prompting, offer one of the following suggestions:

  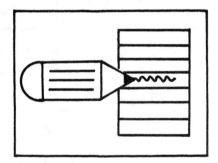

7. Distribute copies of a DoodleLoop to the children. Tell them to use their imaginations, turn the page in any direction they wish, and create their own pictures. Encourage them to take their time, work carefully, and come up with their own unique ideas. Discourage children from making abstract designs. You may wish to suggest that the children's drawings remain secret until sharing time in order to discourage copying.

Initial pencil sketches are fine, but the final picture should be done in crayon.

Published by Good Apple © 1994, Sandy Baker

GA1483

8. It is very important to encourage the children as they tackle this first DoodleLoop. It is helpful to circulate throughout the class as the children draw, offering praise for all attempts.

9. When all drawings are completed, have the class share their creations. Focus the children's attention on drawings which are especially detailed and unique.

10. Display all drawings if possible.

Daily Usage and Expectations

1. In order to develop and stimulate the children's ability to think creatively, it is suggested that one DoodleLoop be given daily.

2. It is important to continually encourage the children to:

   • think of many possibilities before beginning to draw

   • think of unique ideas

   • add details

   • fill in the page (including a background design)

   • work neatly and carefully

3. At first the children may have difficulty expressing their creativity, and you may see some scribbles. However, continued use and encouragement will yield marked improvement. You will be amazed at the hidden creative talents that lie within your students, and you will be thrilled with the results.

The Importance of Sharing

1. It is essential that the children have a vehicle for sharing their DoodleLoops creations in order to reinforce their ideas, to have support and feedback from their classmates, and to encourage divergent thinking.

2. The children may share their work in a variety of ways. You may choose one or more of the following:

   Daily Sharing: Share the DoodleLoops as a group. If time allows, each child may share his or her DoodleLoop with the class. If not, four or five children may share daily so that over the course of a week, all of the children have had one turn to share.

Published by Good Apple © 1994, Sandy Baker

GA1483

Bulletin Boards: Display some of the more complex and creative DoodleLoops on a special bulletin board, or if space allows display all of the children's DoodleLoops.

Overhead Transparencies: Each day you may wish to have one child make an overhead transparency of the DoodleLoop. After the other children in the group have completed their DoodleLoops, you can share the overhead with the class.

Sharing with Another Class: You may wish to have your class or a group of your students share their DoodleLoops with another classroom.

The Language Connection

1. As the children learn to express themselves creatively through drawing, they will want to communicate their ideas. Just as they enjoy describing their pictures, they should be encouraged to write about them.

2. The oral and written language expectations you have will be based on the grade level you teach and the developmental readiness of your children.

3. If the child is just beginning to develop writing skills, he or she may add letters, words, or short sentences to the DoodleLoop. You may encourage this when the children first begin their DoodleLoops or after they have worked with them for a while.

   When you are ready to begin the writing process, demonstrate to the children how to phonetically spell words. What they hear is what they should write. Correct spelling is not necessary. The children may even write one or two letters on the page, such as *b* or *bt* for boat. Any writing at all should be encouraged.

   Here are some examples of what you may expect from your children.

4. If some of the children or your group as a whole is writing well, the DoodleLoops can serve as the motivation for a story. Elements of good story writing (i.e. composition, punctuation, use of descriptive words) can be taught. For children who need additional paper, a master of lined paper is provided at the back of this book.

   *You may also choose to have some of the children dictate words or sentences which you may write on their papers. This approach should be used only if a child is having a great deal of difficulty expressing his or her thoughts in writing.

Published by Good Apple © 1994. Sandy Baker

GA1483

Family Involvement

1. At the beginning of the year it is helpful to write a letter to each child's family explaining the purpose of the DoodleLoops. A sample letter is provided on page viii.

2. It is very important that the children share their DoodleLoops with their families. They provide a wonderful connection between school and home, and families truly enjoy sharing with their children and watching their progress over the course of the year.

Enjoy the DoodleLoops!
They offer endless possibilities for learning
and for expanding creative awareness!

*For more daily writing activities, try *Writing DoodleLoops*, GA1484. Your emerging writers will love them!

Acknowledgment
My deepest thanks to Donna Napolitano, devoted professional, for her encouragement and continual support.

Dear Family,

This year your child will be working on some very special pages called *Drawing DoodleLoops*. These DoodleLoops are the first step in developing the creative writing process. These work sheets will be used as a tool to stimulate creative thinking. DoodleLoops have proven to be wonderful learning tools. The children love them and truly enjoy working on them every day.

The children begin with a shape, line, or object drawn on a page, and they enhance the drawing and make it into their own original "creation." For example, a shape may be enhanced as follows:

**Original
Shape**   **Possibilities**

Your child may also begin to write or dictate short sentences related to the DoodleLoops. Please encourage these first attempts at writing, but remember that writing is not necessary at this point.

Please take time to discuss and share these special pages with your child when they are brought home. Thank you so much for your cooperation, involvement, and support.

Sincerely,

Published by Good Apple © 1994, Sandy Baker GA1483

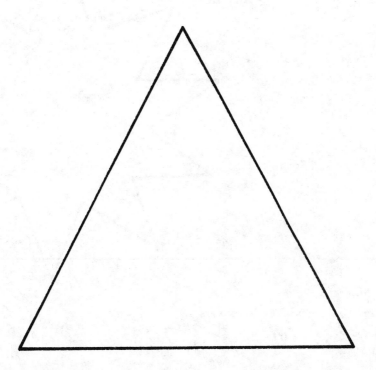

GA1483

GA1483

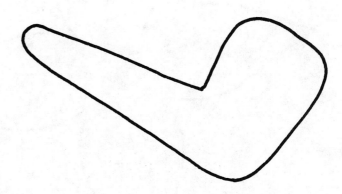

GA1483

GA1483

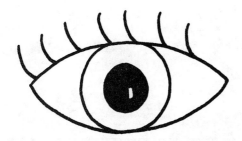

GA1483

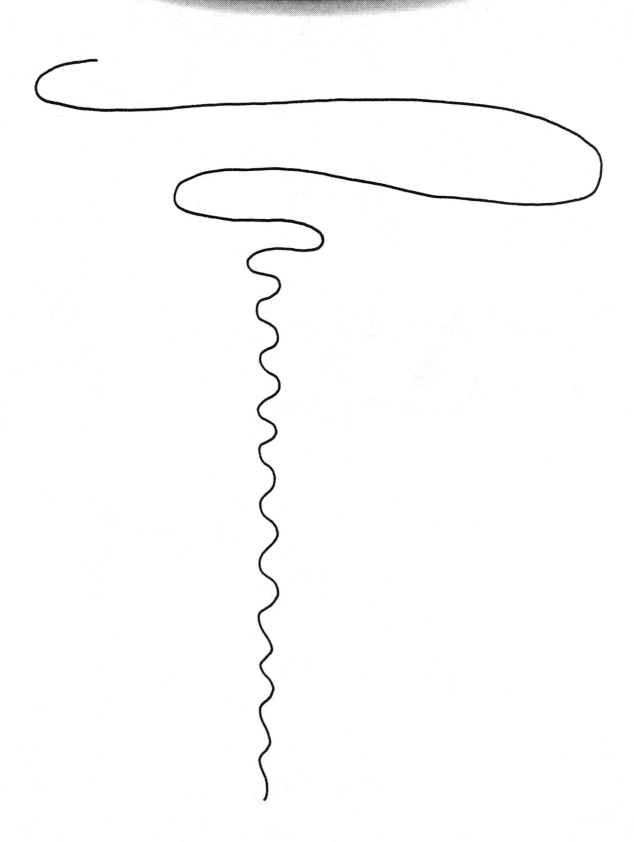

GA1483

 GA1483

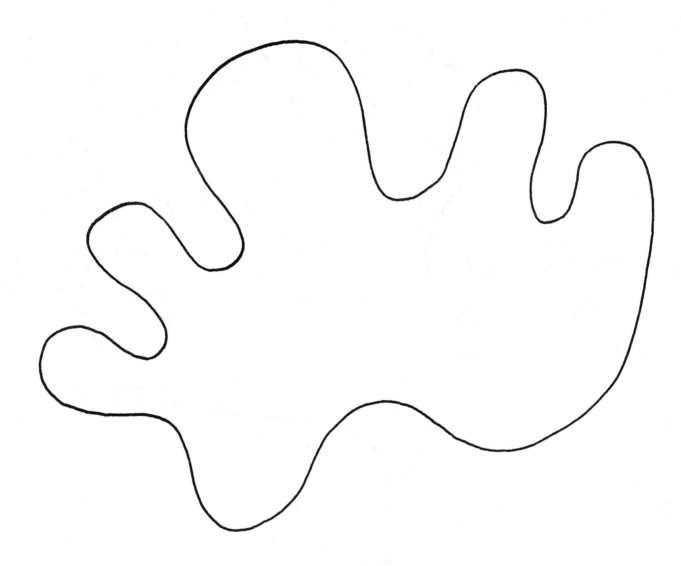

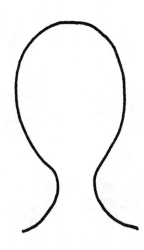

GA1483

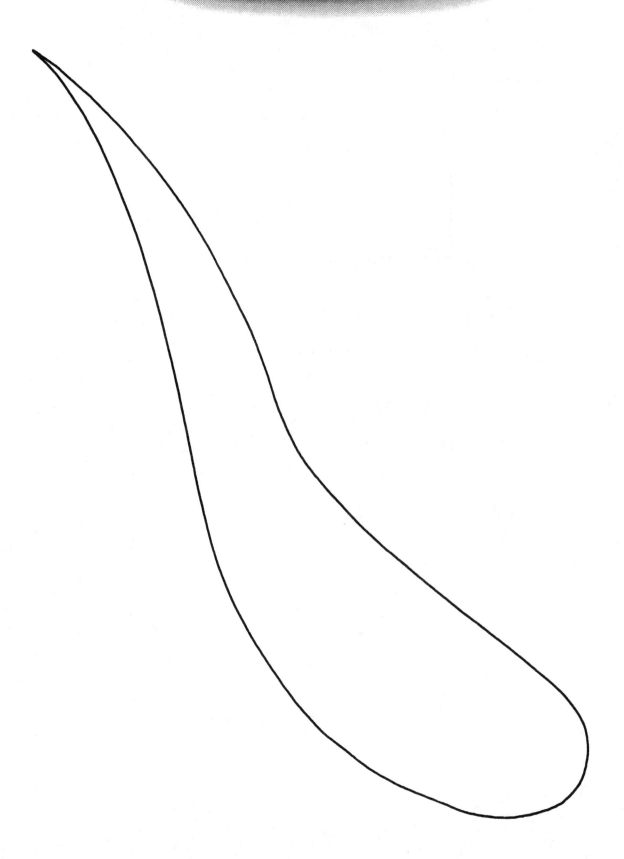

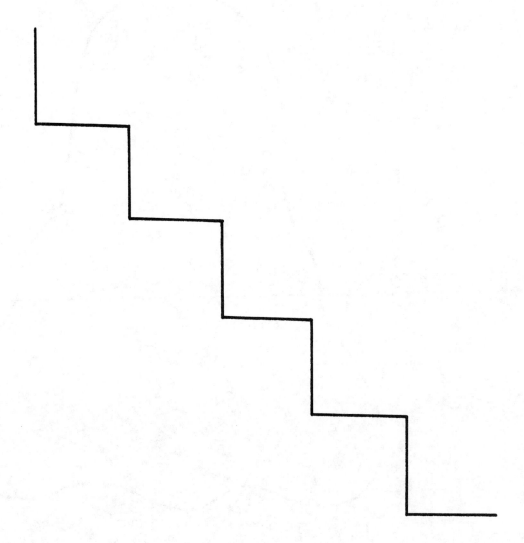

GA1483

GA1483

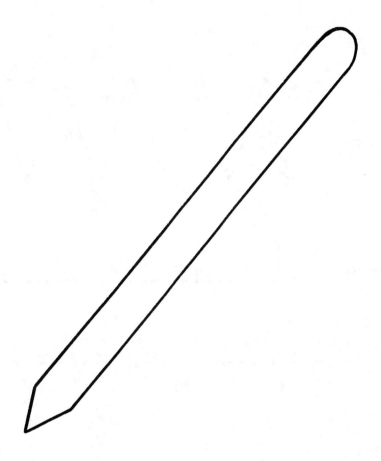

Published by Good Apple © 1994, Sandy Baker

GA1483

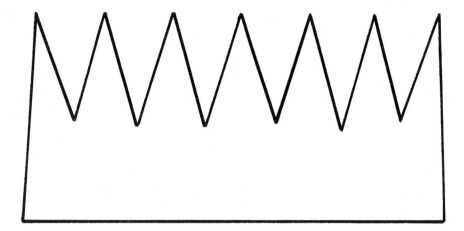

GA1483

Published by Good Apple © 1994. Sandy Baker

GA1483

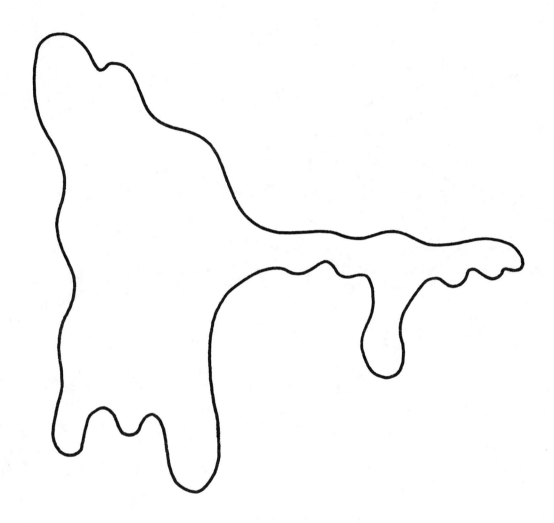

GA1483

Published by Good Apple © 1994, Sandy Baker

GA1483

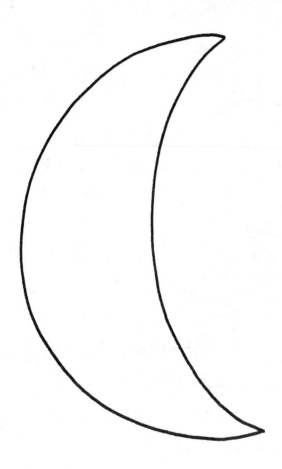

Published by Good Apple © 1994, Sandy Baker

GA1483

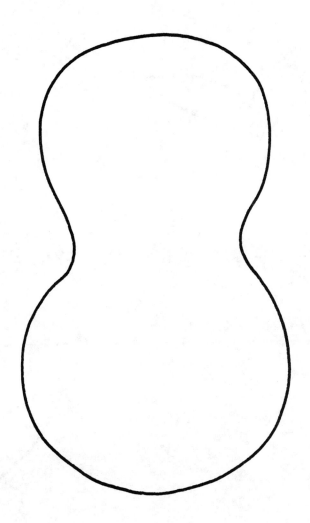

GA1483

Published by Good Apple © 1994, Sandy Baker

GA1483

Published by Good Apple © 1994, Sandy Baker

GA1483

GA1483

 GA1483

GA1483

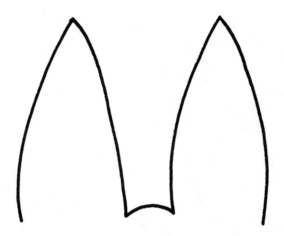

GA1483

GA1483

GA1483

Published by Good Apple © 1994, Sandy Baker GA1483

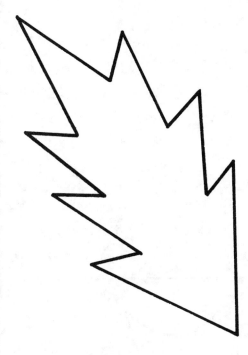

GA1483

GA1483

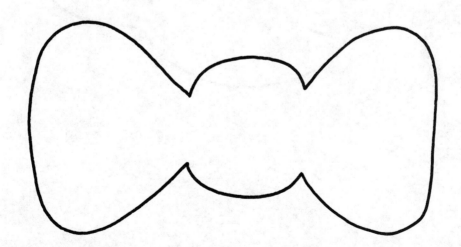

Published by Good Apple © 1994. Sandy Baker

GA1483

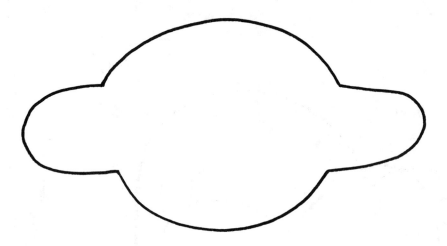

GA1483

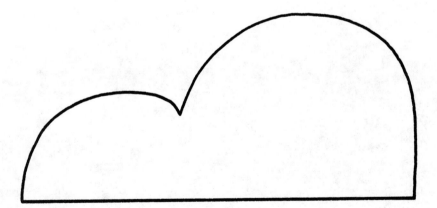

Published by Good Apple © 1994, Sandy Baker GA1483

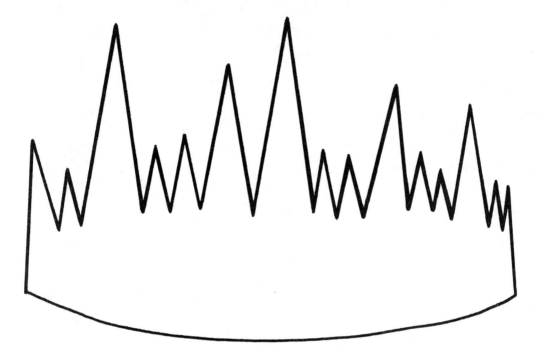

Published by Good Apple © 1994. Sandy Baker

GA1483

GA1483

GA1483

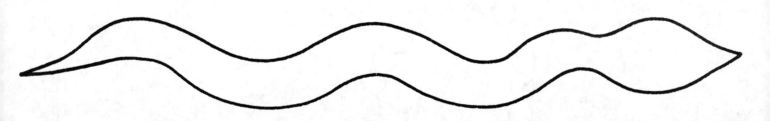

GA1483

GA1483

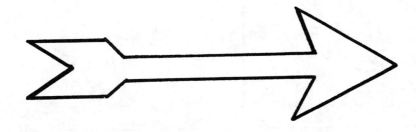

Published by Good Apple © 1994, Sandy Baker

GA1483

42

GA1483

GA1483

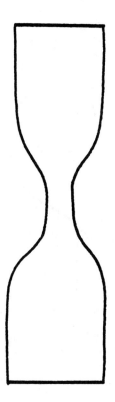

GA1483

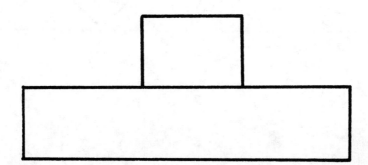

Published by Good Apple © 1994, Sandy Baker

GA1483

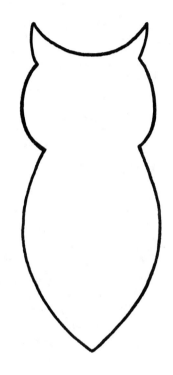

Published by Good Apple © 1994, Sandy Baker

GA1483

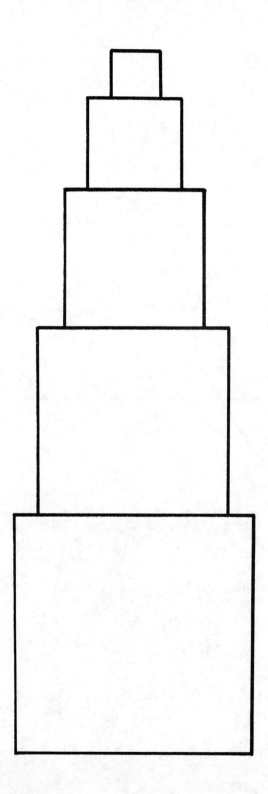

GA1483

Published by Good Apple © 1994, Sandy Baker

GA1483

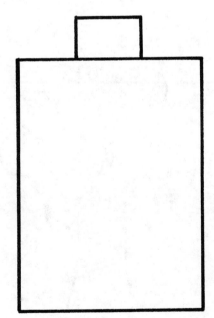

GA1483

GA1483

51

GA1483

Published by Good Apple © 1994, Sandy Baker

GA1483

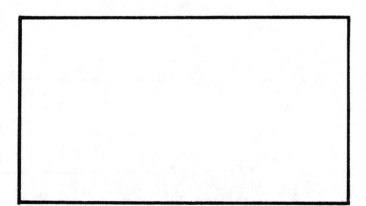

GA1483

Published by Good Apple © 1994, Sandy Baker

GA1483

GA1483

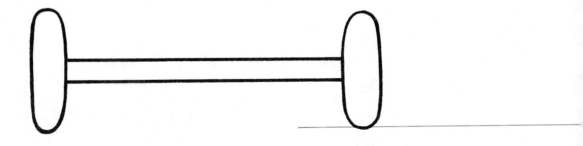

Published by Good Apple © 1994, Sandy Baker

GA1483

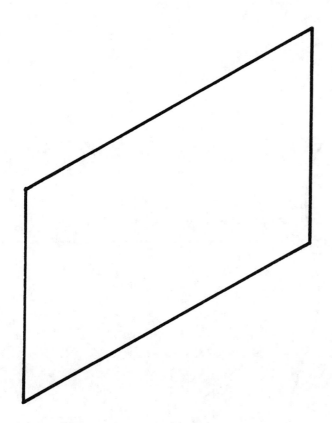

Published by Good Apple © 1994, Sandy Baker

GA1483

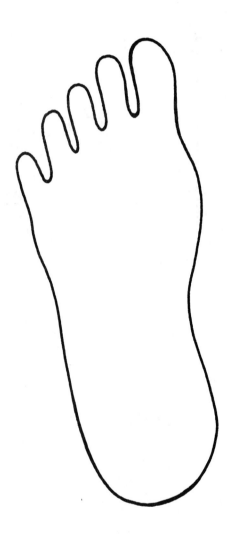

GA1483

GA1483

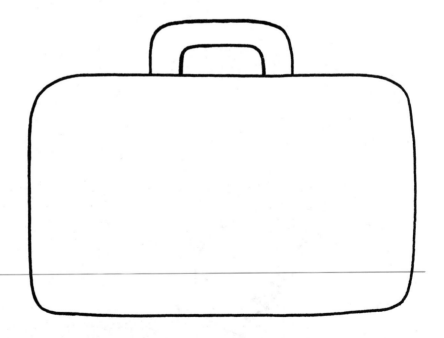

GA1483

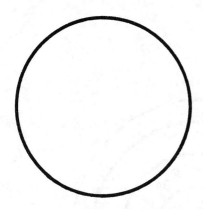

GA1483

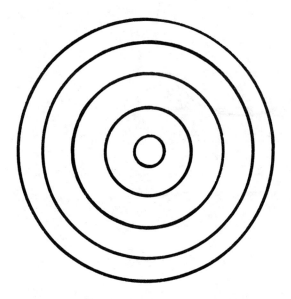

 GA1483

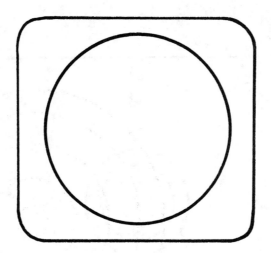

GA1483

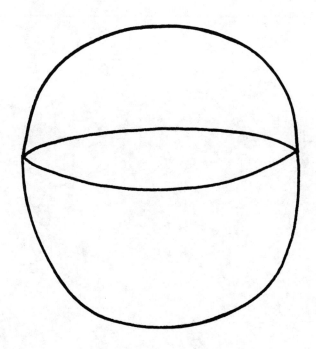

GA1483

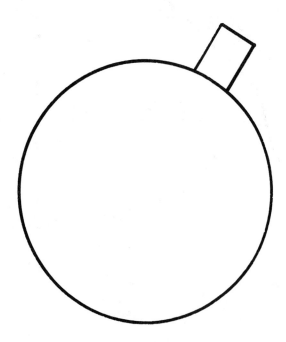

GA1483

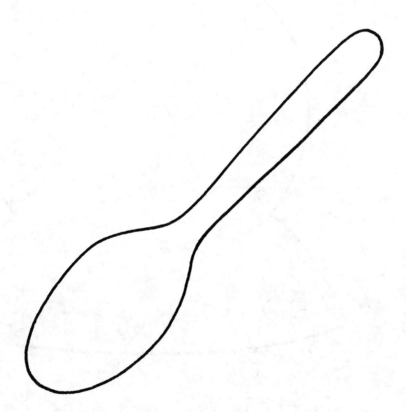

GA1483

GA1483

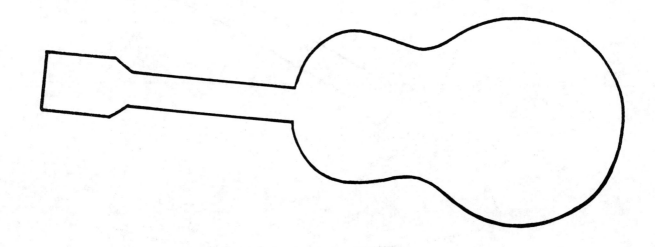

Published by Good Apple © 1994, Sandy Baker

GA1483

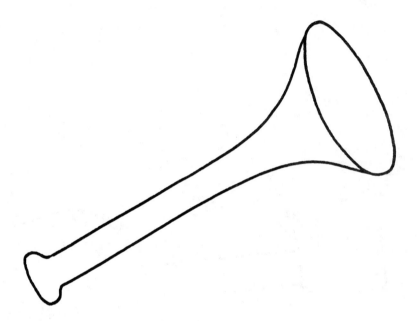

GA1483

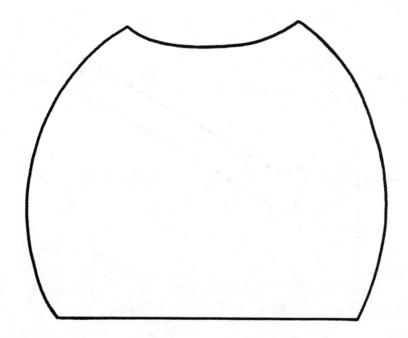

Published by Good Apple © 1994, Sandy Baker GA1483

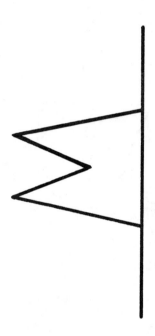

GA1483

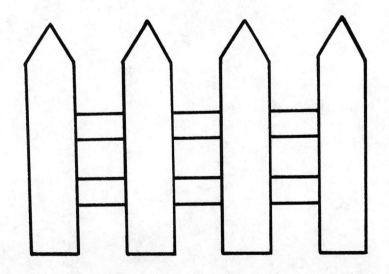

Published by Good Apple © 1994, Sandy Baker

GA1483

Published by Good Apple © 1994, Sandy Baker

GA1483

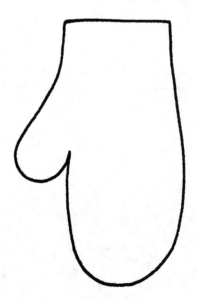

GA1483

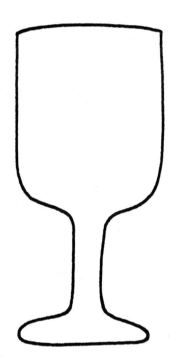

GA1483

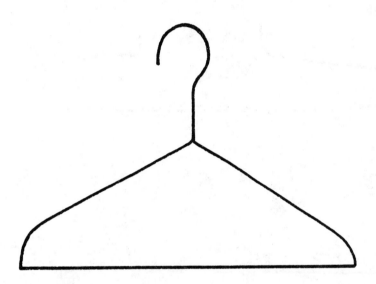

Published by Good Apple © 1994, Sandy Baker

GA1483

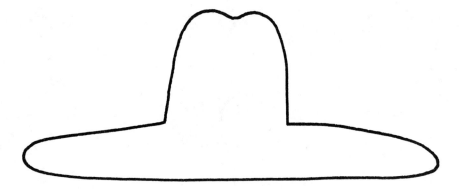

GA1483

GA1483

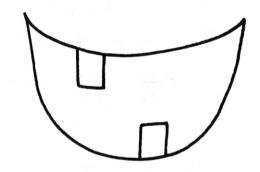

GA1483

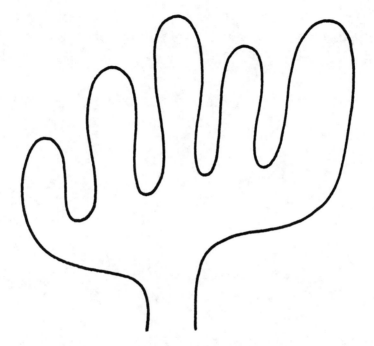

Published by Good Apple © 1994, Sandy Baker

GA1483

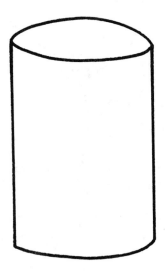

Published by Good Apple © 1994, Sandy Baker

GA1483

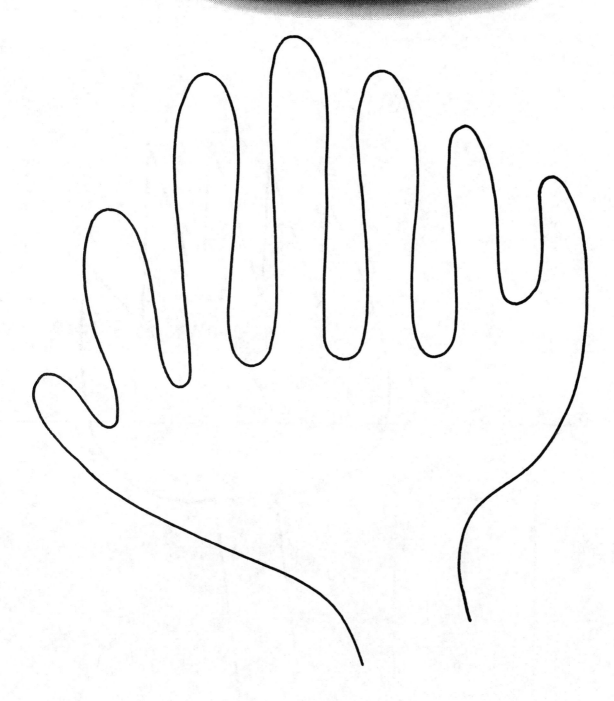

GA1483

GA1483

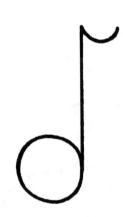

GA1483

GA1483

GA1483